P9-CBC-836

DRAW OR PASTE
A PICTURE OF YOURSELF HERE.

Melrose Public Library

DISCARDED

CHILDREN'S ROOM
MELROSE PUBLIC LIBRARY

THIS IS ME.
AND THIS IS MY BOOK.
EVERYBODY ELSE KEEP OUT!

648
(Childhood Resource Library)

Text copyright © 1980, 1999 by Ann Banks and Nancy Evans
Illustrations copyright © 1999 by True Kelley

All rights reserved. No part of this book may be reproduced or transmitted in any form or by any means, electronic or mechanical, including photocopying, recording, or by any information storage and retrieval system, without permission in writing from the publisher.

Published by Crown Publishers, Inc., a Random House company, 201 East 50th Street, New York, New York 10022.
Originally published in a different form by Harmony Books, a division of Crown Publishers, Inc., in 1980.

CROWN is a trademark of Crown Publishers, Inc.

www.randomhouse.com/kids

Printed in the United States of America

Library of Congress Cataloging-in-Publication Data

Banks, Ann.
Goodbye, house / by Ann Banks and Nancy Evans ; illustrations by True Kelley.
p. cm.
Summary: Suggests activities and projects to help in adjusting to the move to a new house,
including the recording of favorite memories, planning the move, and listing likes and dislikes about the new house.
ISBN 0-517-88574-3 (trade pbk.)
1. Moving, Household—Juvenile literature. [1. Moving, Household.] I. Evans, Nancy (Nancy B.) II. Kelley, True, ill. III. Title.
TX307.B36   1999
648'.9—dc21   98-35995

10 9 8 7 6 5 4 3 2 1

A KIDS' GUIDE TO MOVING

GOODBYE, HOUSE

by ANN BANKS and NANCY EVANS

illustrations by TRUE KELLEY

CROWN PUBLISHERS, INC. ♕ NEW YORK

THIS IS YOUR BOOK

Your parents have told you you're going to move. Maybe you hate the idea, or maybe you're looking forward to it. However you feel, the next few months can be a confusing time. Your parents will be busy making plans for the move and for your new home. There will be many things on your mind. You may feel left out. You may wonder why you have to go at all. After all, this move wasn't your idea. You'll be sad to leave your friends, and you won't want to forget them. You may be wondering what your new school will be like and how soon you'll be able to make new friends.

Goodbye, House is a place where you can make your own plans for the move. There are projects in *Goodbye, House* to begin right now, projects to do as you get ready for the move, and projects to complete while you're getting settled in your new home.

GOODBYE, HOUSE

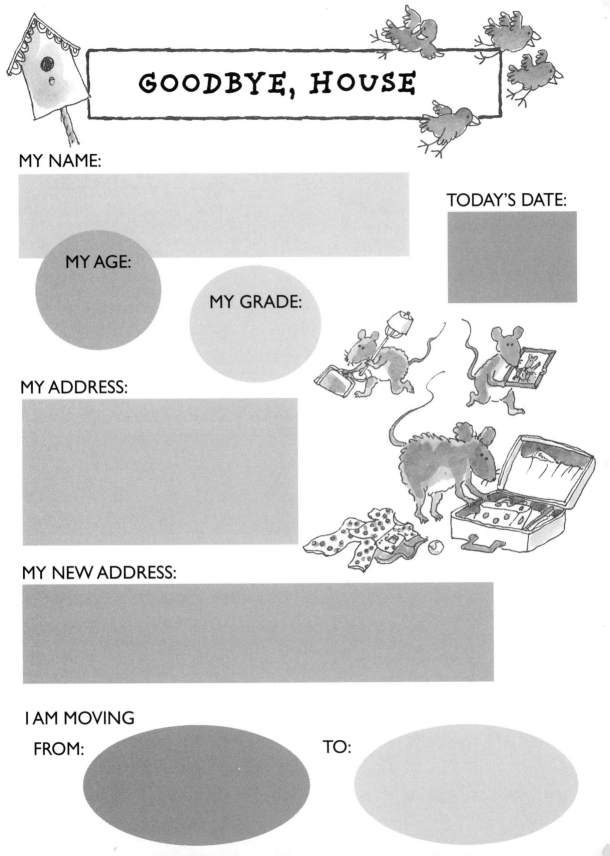

MY NAME:

TODAY'S DATE:

MY AGE:

MY GRADE:

MY ADDRESS:

MY NEW ADDRESS:

I AM MOVING

FROM:

TO:

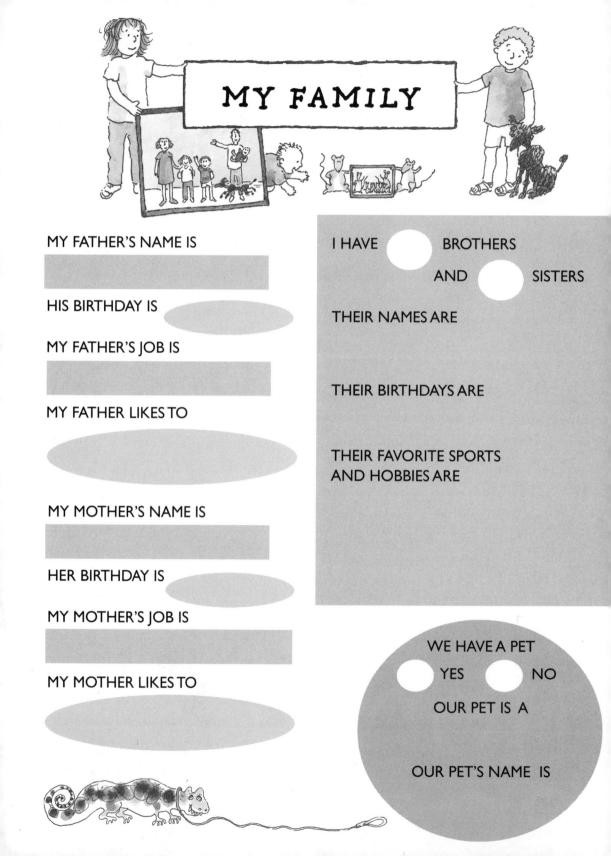

MY FAMILY

MY FATHER'S NAME IS

HIS BIRTHDAY IS

MY FATHER'S JOB IS

MY FATHER LIKES TO

MY MOTHER'S NAME IS

HER BIRTHDAY IS

MY MOTHER'S JOB IS

MY MOTHER LIKES TO

I HAVE ◯ BROTHERS

AND ◯ SISTERS

THEIR NAMES ARE

THEIR BIRTHDAYS ARE

THEIR FAVORITE SPORTS
AND HOBBIES ARE

WE HAVE A PET

◯ YES ◯ NO

OUR PET IS A

OUR PET'S NAME IS

GETTING READY TO MOVE

Draw or paste a picture of your old house here.

ADDRESS:

MY FAVORITE MEMORIES

There are things you'll want to remember after you've moved. The time you hit a home run. The play you put on with your friends. The place you learned to swim. The time you went to an amusement park. Your favorite picnic spot. A special tree. So you don't forget, write your favorite memories here.

I REMEMBER

I REMEMBER

I REMEMBER

I REMEMBER

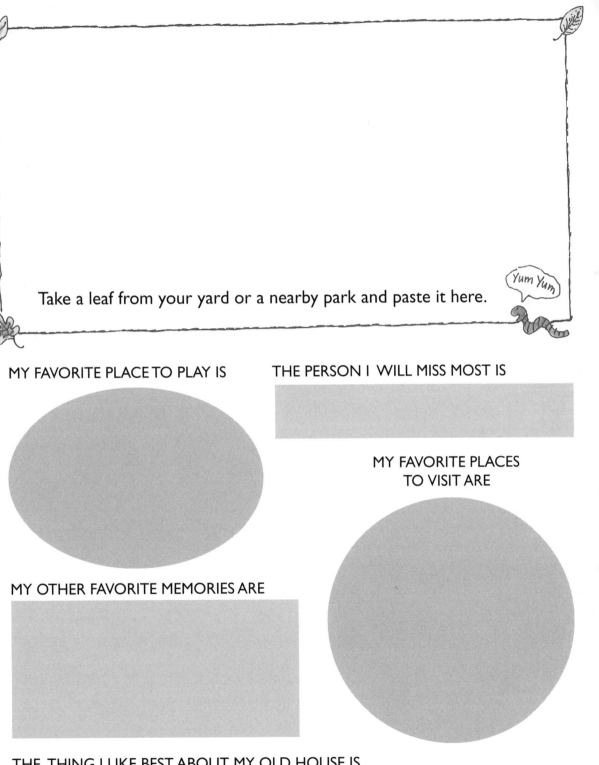

Take a leaf from your yard or a nearby park and paste it here.

Yum Yum

MY FAVORITE PLACE TO PLAY IS

THE PERSON I WILL MISS MOST IS

MY FAVORITE PLACES
TO VISIT ARE

MY OTHER FAVORITE MEMORIES ARE

THE THING I LIKE BEST ABOUT MY OLD HOUSE IS

MY FAVORITE PLACES AND PEOPLE

On these two pages, draw or paste pictures of your favorite places and people.

HOW I FEEL ABOUT MOVING

Your feelings may change as moving day gets closer. They will probably change again after you first move into your new home, and again after you've been in your new town or neighborhood for a few weeks. Return to this page whenever you want to write down your feelings. Put the date next to each entry.

SECRET TREASURE

So that your old home won't forget you, bury something in your yard or a favorite place. Make it something that is special to you.... Your lucky stone. A marble. A pine cone. Seashells. A picture you've drawn. Put a piece of paper with your name and age in a jar or box. Bury that with your treasure. **On this page, draw a map showing where your treasure is buried.** You may want to come back and dig it up someday.

TIP: Find out who is moving into the house you're leaving. If the family has children about your age, make a list of the things that are fun to do in your neighborhood and the kids they might like to meet. Wish them a nice stay in your old home.

MY FRIENDS

Ask your favorite friends for their pictures to paste here. Fill in each friend's name and birthday next to the picture. Be sure to get their addresses, phone numbers, and e-mail addresses, so you can stay in touch after the move.

NAME:

BIRTHDAY:

ADDRESS:

paste photo here

PHONE NUMBER:

E-MAIL ADDRESS:

MY FRIEND'S FAVORITE THINGS:

★ TV SHOW: ★ COMPUTER GAME:

★ BOOK: ★ MOVIE STAR: ★ SPORT:

Tip: Ask your mother or father to get you pre-stamped postcards, and then write your name and your new address on them. Give them to your friends so they can write to you at your new home.

NAME:

BIRTHDAY:

ADDRESS:

paste photo here

PHONE NUMBER:

E-MAIL ADDRESS:

MY FRIEND'S FAVORITE THINGS:

★ TV SHOW: ★ COMPUTER GAME:

★ BOOK: ★ MOVIE STAR: ★ SPORT:

NAME:

BIRTHDAY:

ADDRESS:

paste photo here

PHONE NUMBER:

E-MAIL ADDRESS:

MY FRIEND'S FAVORITE THINGS:

★ TV SHOW: ★ COMPUTER GAME:

★ BOOK: ★ MOVIE STAR: ★ SPORT:

GOODBYE, FRIENDS

Who are the people to whom you want to be sure to say goodbye? You don't want to forget anybody important. Write in the names of the people you might like to see before you leave. Put a check mark beside each name after you say goodbye.

MY TEACHER:

GOODBYE TO

MY BEST FRIENDS:

GOODBYE TO

GOODBYE TO

GOODBYE TO

MY FAVORITE NEIGHBORS:

GOODBYE TO

GOODBYE TO

GOODBYE TO

OTHER SPECIAL PEOPLE:

GOODBYE TO

GOODBYE TO

GOODBYE TO

MY BABY-SITTER:

GOODBYE TO

Tip: See if you can have a goodbye party. Ask all your friends to bring you something to remember them by—a snapshot of themselves, their favorite joke written on a piece of paper, a baseball card.

GOODBYE, OLD SCHOOL

NAME OF MY SCHOOL:

MY TEACHER'S NAME:

HOW I GET TO SCHOOL:

FAVORITE AFTER-SCHOOL ACTIVITY AT MY SCHOOL:

MOST POPULAR SPORT AT MY SCHOOL:

NUMBER OF KIDS IN MY CLASS:

NUMBER OF GIRLS:

NUMBER OF BOYS:

Draw or paste a picture of your old school here.

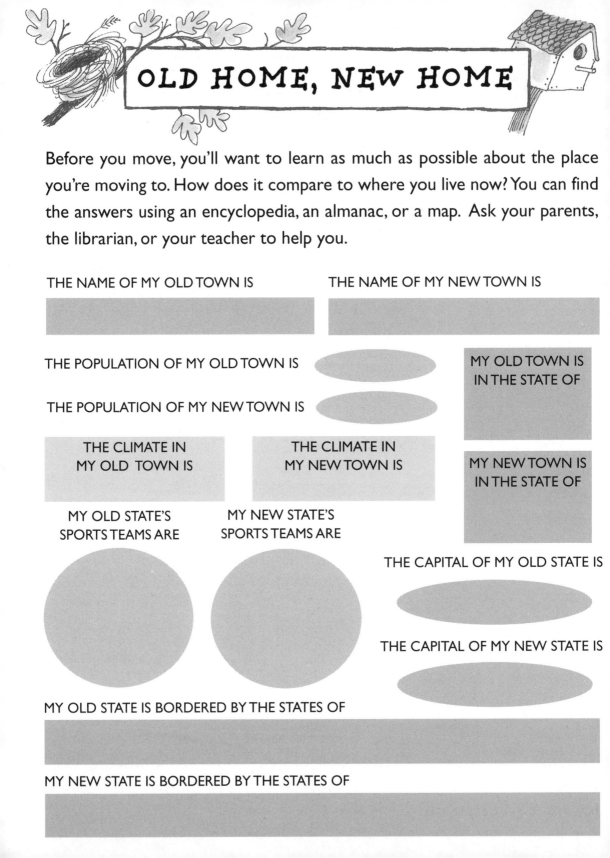

OLD HOME, NEW HOME

Before you move, you'll want to learn as much as possible about the place you're moving to. How does it compare to where you live now? You can find the answers using an encyclopedia, an almanac, or a map. Ask your parents, the librarian, or your teacher to help you.

THE NAME OF MY OLD TOWN IS

THE NAME OF MY NEW TOWN IS

THE POPULATION OF MY OLD TOWN IS

THE POPULATION OF MY NEW TOWN IS

MY OLD TOWN IS IN THE STATE OF

THE CLIMATE IN MY OLD TOWN IS

THE CLIMATE IN MY NEW TOWN IS

MY NEW TOWN IS IN THE STATE OF

MY OLD STATE'S SPORTS TEAMS ARE

MY NEW STATE'S SPORTS TEAMS ARE

THE CAPITAL OF MY OLD STATE IS

THE CAPITAL OF MY NEW STATE IS

MY OLD STATE IS BORDERED BY THE STATES OF

MY NEW STATE IS BORDERED BY THE STATES OF

GOOD RIDDANCE!

Thank goodness! Finally you'll be rid of all those things you hate. What will you be glad to leave behind? A nickname you can't stand? Silly rules at school? The bully on the block? The mess in your room?

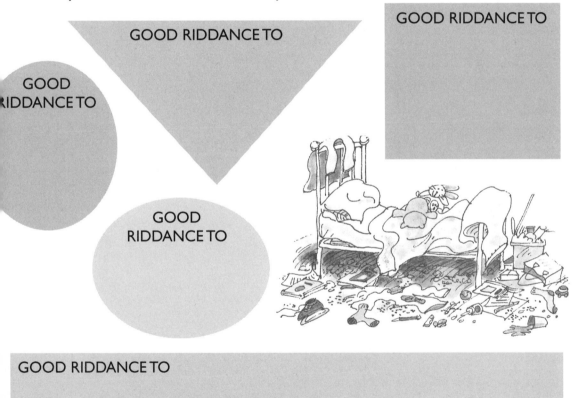

GOOD RIDDANCE TO

GOOD RIDDANCE TO

GOOD RIDDANCE TO

GOOD RIDDANCE TO

GOOD RIDDANCE TO

Tip: Before you move, you might want to give some of your old toys or books to the Salvation Army or to a children's hospital. Sit down with your parents and decide what you want to give away and to whom it should go. Or ask if you can have a yard sale to sell the things you don't want to take to your new house or apartment.

I CAN'T WAIT

What are you looking forward to after you move? Maybe you'll get to ride a bus to school. Maybe you'll be near a park with a wonderful playground. Maybe you'll be near a beach. Maybe you'll finally have a room of your own. Maybe there's a good climbing tree nearby. Maybe you'll live in an apartment building with an elevator.

Ask your mom or dad what new things you'll get to do and see in your new town. Write them down here.

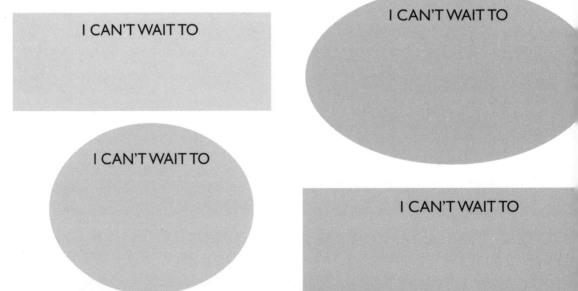

I CAN'T WAIT TO

I CAN'T WAIT TO

I CAN'T WAIT TO

I CAN'T WAIT TO

WORRIES

Any move will bring a lot of changes for you and your family. Some you'll be looking forward to. Others may be scary. It helps to remember that you aren't the only one who's ever had to move. Millions of families move every year. Here are some of the things that other kids have worried about. If you have any of these worries, you'll feel better if you talk them over with your parents or a friend before the move.

★ What if nobody talks to you the first day of school?

★ What if your birthday comes soon after the move? Will you have any new friends to help you celebrate?

★ What if your teacher doesn't like you?

★ What if you don't get invited to any parties?

★ What if you're moving farther away from your grandparents and other family members? When will you see them again?

★ What if your clothes are different from what all the other kids wear?

★ What if you're behind in school?

★ What if you're moving to a smaller home? Will you still be able to have friends stay over?

★ What if your new school's so big you get lost?

★ What if you have to leave your pet behind?
(If you think about this ahead of time, you can make sure your pet will have a good new home.)

A NEW START

Imagine that you've already moved. What do you want your new life to be like? Are there things about yourself you'd like to change, ways that you'd like things to be different?

I'LL BE GOOD!

I WILL TRY TO

I WILL TRY **NOT** TO

I don't see my good old litter box!

Tip: After you move, your pet will probably be able to tell that things are different. Give him special attention when you get to your new home so he doesn't get upset. Pet him a lot or take him for walks. If you have to leave a pet behind, give the new owners a postcard with your new address on it. Ask them to write and tell you how your pet is doing. You also might want to make a scrapbook introducing your pet to its new owner.

MY NEW ROOM

Ask your parents what your new room will look like.

How many windows will there be?

Will you be sharing your room?

If so, whom will you be sharing it with?

If so, will you have bunk beds?

What color are the walls in your new room?

If you could paint your new room any color, what would it be?

What will you put on the walls? A poster of your favorite TV, sports, or rock star? A baseball pennant? Snapshots of your friends? Make a list.

You'll feel better if you can fix up your room right away. So start thinking now about where you will put your favorite things.

Will you have a desk?

Will you have a bookcase?

Will you be getting anything new especially for your new room?

What will it be?

HELPING OUT

You can get ready to move by

★ HELPING WITH BROTHERS AND SISTERS.

★ RETURNING BOOKS TO THE LIBRARY.

★ DECIDING WHICH TOYS YOU DON'T WANT ANYMORE AND GIVING THEM AWAY.

★ RUNNING ERRANDS FOR YOUR PARENTS.

★ CLEANING OUT YOUR SCHOOL LOCKER.

Tip: Remember that your parents are leaving their home and friends, too. Surprise them by doing nice things. If you bring your mother a glass of lemonade while she's packing, both of you will feel better.

Other ways to help are:

1.

2.

3.

4.

5.

Tip: If you're going to be around the day the movers come, find out ahead of time what you can do to help. Maybe you want to offer to run last-minute errands for your parents. Maybe you'd rather spend the day saying goodbye to your friends.

PLANNING MY TRIP

Ask your mom or dad about plans for the trip and write down the answers here.

WHO WILL BE MAKING THE TRIP WITH YOU?

WHAT DAY WILL
THE MOVING VAN COME?

WHAT DAY WILL YOU LEAVE?

HOW WILL YOU TRAVEL?

(CAR, BUS, TRAIN, PLANE)

WILL YOU STAY IN A MOTEL?

HOW MANY NIGHTS?

HOW MANY STATES WILL
YOU GO THROUGH?

HOW MANY MILES WILL YOU TRAVEL?

HOW LONG WILL IT TAKE?

Just before you move, send a welcoming postcard
to yourself at your new home.

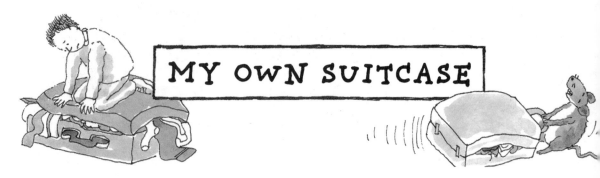

MY OWN SUITCASE

What do you want to take? Pretend you are already on your way, and think of what you'd like with you on the trip. Think of what you'll want for the first night in your new house, too.

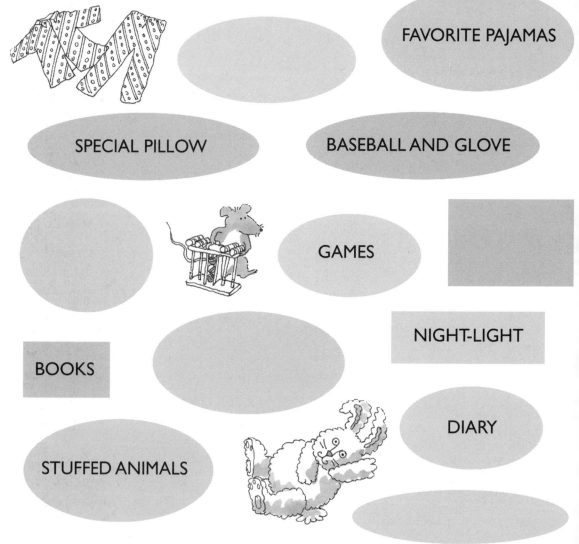

FAVORITE PAJAMAS

SPECIAL PILLOW

BASEBALL AND GLOVE

GAMES

NIGHT-LIGHT

BOOKS

DIARY

STUFFED ANIMALS

MY TRIP TO
MY NEW HOUSE

Draw or paste a picture of your
family on moving day here.

ARE WE THERE YET?

Be sure to take *Goodbye, House* with you on moving day so you can keep a record of the trip.

MY TRIP RECORD

DATE(S) OF THE TRIP:

WE ARE TRAVELING FROM   TO

THE TRIP WILL TAKE   HOURS/DAYS.

WE LEFT AT   O'CLOCK.

WE ARE TRAVELING BY

WE PLAYED THESE GAMES:

WE SANG THESE SONGS:

WE ARRIVED AT   O'CLOCK ON

HERE ARE THE PLACES WE SAW:

WE SPENT THE NIGHT AT

MY NEW HOME

Draw or paste a picture of your new house here.

ADDRESS:

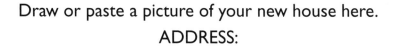

Tip: So that your magazines arrive at your new home, change the address for your magazine subscriptions several weeks before you move.

WE'RE HERE!

Hello, house! Now that you've arrived at your new home, you'll want to learn your way around as soon as you can.

★ The first thing to do is find your room.

★ Make a sign with your name on it to put on the door.

★ Bring your suitcase to your room.

★ Look out your windows. What do you see?

★ Look up and down the street.
See if there are any bicycles or skateboards.

★ Ask your parents what you can do to help.

★ You might want to save a box from the movers to make a playhouse.

★ Ask for a flashlight so you can find your way around in the dark.

★ Look for a good route to walk your dog.

Tip: When you get to your new home, refer to your trip record and write postcards to your old friends telling them about your trip and your arrival.

MY NEW NEIGHBORHOOD

Draw a picture or a map of your new neighborhood, showing where you live and all the places you like to go. Find a secret hiding place in your new home. Do **not** put your secret hiding place on this map.

THE NIGHT BEFORE MY FIRST DAY OF SCHOOL

★ What time will you leave for school? ___ o'clock

★ How will you get there? Bus Walk Car

Will anyone be coming with you? yes no

Who? ___

★ Will you be going to the same school as any of your brothers or sisters?

yes no

★ Will you bring your own lunch?

yes no

★ What other things will you take with you? Make a list of what you'll need for school. Then put the things together in one pile.

★ What will you wear? List the clothes you'll be wearing and put them out for tomorrow morning.

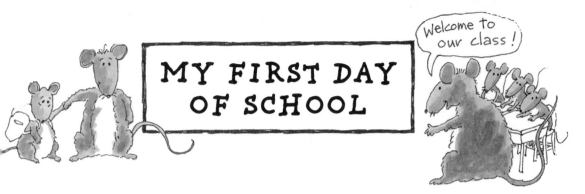

MY FIRST DAY OF SCHOOL

Welcome to our class!

Write down how you felt about the first day of school.

HELLO, NEW SCHOOL

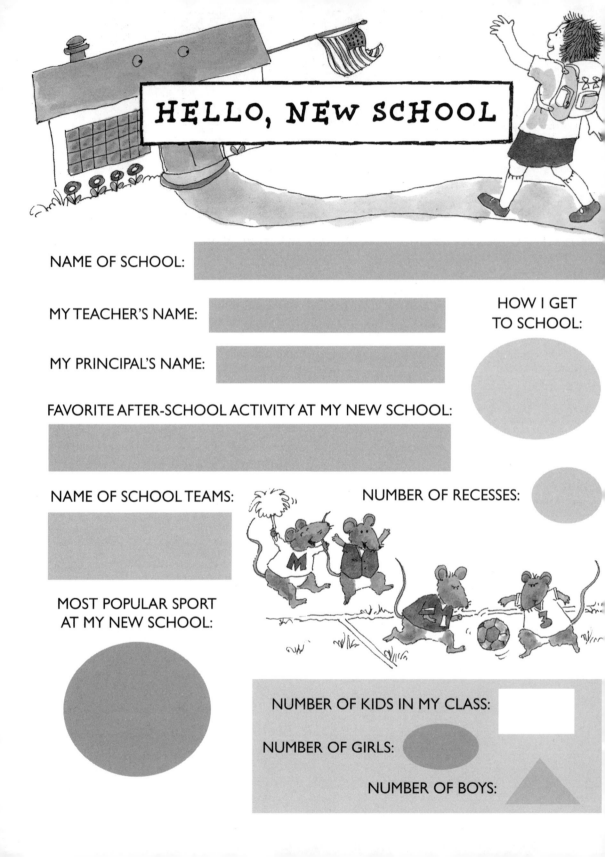

NAME OF SCHOOL:

MY TEACHER'S NAME:

MY PRINCIPAL'S NAME:

HOW I GET TO SCHOOL:

FAVORITE AFTER-SCHOOL ACTIVITY AT MY NEW SCHOOL:

NAME OF SCHOOL TEAMS:

NUMBER OF RECESSES:

MOST POPULAR SPORT AT MY NEW SCHOOL:

NUMBER OF KIDS IN MY CLASS:

NUMBER OF GIRLS:

NUMBER OF BOYS:

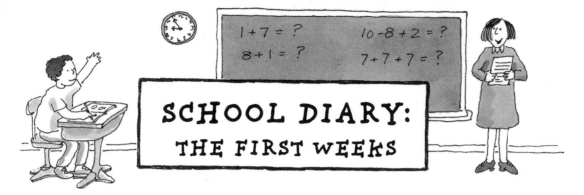

SCHOOL DIARY:
THE FIRST WEEKS

There will probably be some things about your new school that you like and some things you can't stand. You may be ahead in some subjects and behind in others. There will be new school rules to learn. Your new classmates may wear different clothes and play different games.

At first, everything may seem so different that you feel scared. But after a while, you'll begin to feel more at home. On these next pages, you can write down what you see, hear, and feel during the first weeks at your new school.

YOUR CLASSROOM

ARE THE DESKS ARRANGED   IN A CIRCLE OR
                                              IN ROWS?

WHO SITS NEXT TO YOU?

ARE THERE DIFFERENT RULES?
WHAT ARE THEY?

WHAT DOES YOUR NEW CLASSROOM HAVE THAT YOUR OLD ONE DIDN'T?

YOUR SCHOOL

DOES YOUR SCHOOL PLAYGROUND HAVE THESE?

SWINGS YES NO   BASEBALL DIAMOND YES NO

BASKETBALL HOOP YES NO

CHECK WHICH GAMES YOU PLAY:

○ JUMP ROPE   ○ BASKETBALL   ○ BASEBALL

OTHER:

WHAT DO YOU LIKE BEST ABOUT YOUR NEW SCHOOL?

WHAT DO YOU LIKE LEAST ABOUT YOUR NEW SCHOOL?

SCHOOLWORK:

IS THERE MORE HOMEWORK
THAN AT YOUR OLD SCHOOL?

YES   NO   HOW LONG DOES IT TAKE YOU TO DO IT?

ARE THERE SUBJECTS
YOU'RE AHEAD IN?   YES   NO
WHAT ARE THEY?

WHAT IS YOUR FAVORITE SUBJECT?

WHAT IS YOUR LEAST FAVORITE SUBJECT?

ARE THERE SUBJECTS
YOU'RE BEHIND IN?   YES   NO
WHAT ARE THEY?

ARE THERE CLUBS IN YOUR SCHOOL
THAT DO INTERESTING THINGS?

YES   NO

WHICH ONES WILL YOU JOIN?

DO YOU HAVE ANY SUBJECTS IN YOUR NEW SCHOOL
THAT YOU DIDN'T HAVE IN YOUR OLD SCHOOL?   YES   NO

WHAT ARE THEY?

CLASSMATES:

HOW DO KIDS DRESS AT YOUR NEW SCHOOL?

HOW IS THE WAY THEY DRESS DIFFERENT
FROM THE WAY YOUR OLD FRIENDS DRESSED?

HOW DO YOU FEEL DIFFERENT
FROM THE KIDS IN THE CLASS?

HELLO, FRIENDS

Your new classmates will want to know about you, too. They'll want to know about your family, where you live, and what you think about your new town and school. They'll want to know what you like to do and what you're good at. Underline the activities you can do. Put two lines under those you're really good at.

★ PLAY COMPUTER GAMES

WHAT IS YOUR FAVORITE GAME?

★ PLAY A SPORT

WHAT SPORTS DO YOU PLAY?

★ PLAY A MUSICAL INSTRUMENT

WHAT INSTRUMENT DO YOU PLAY?

★ ACT   ★ SING

★ DRAW CARTOONS

WHAT IS YOUR FAVORITE PIECE TO PLAY?   ★ DO GYMNASTICS

★ DO CARD TRICKS

★ MAKE CANDY OR COOKIES

OTHER THINGS I CAN DO ARE:

★ DO PUPPET SHOWS

WHAT I DON'T LIKE ABOUT MY NEW HOME

I don't like

WHAT I LIKE ABOUT
MY NEW HOME

I like

GOODBYE, HOUSE:
A PARENTS' GUIDE

It's never easy being the new kid on the block. *Goodbye, House* invites your child to express and order his feelings as he chronicles the family move in his very own book. It engages the child in activities from the moment he is first told about the impending move. As he fills in the book, the child will gain a sense of mastery over the new environment and the feeling of overwhelming newness will diminish. Once the adjustment is completed, *Goodbye, House* will serve as a scrapbook that can be reviewed fondly.

The most important function of *Goodbye, House* is as a diary in which the child can feel free to express herself as the move approaches. By writing down what she feels when she first hears about the move, and again around moving day, and later when she arrives in the new place, she will be able to acknowledge and clarify the range of emotions she passes through. She will also be better able to talk about her feelings with you.

We suggest you take the time now to read *Goodbye, House* before your child begins to fill it in, so you'll know what questions your child will be likely to ask in the weeks ahead. The following pages offer general suggestions to help you make the move easier for your child, and specific suggestions to help your child use *Goodbye, House*.

★ **Tell your child as soon as possible about the move.** You might think it would be best to hold off until the last moment, but children can usually sense when something's going on. So think of the early announcement as giving your child time to adjust rather than time to worry. What you don't want is for your child to hear about the move from neighbors or friends before hearing it from you.

★ **Be honest about the reason for the move.** When the move is a matter of choice—for instance, to take a new job or because of a promotion—many parents like to bring their children into the discussion to ask how they feel about it.

If the move is necessitated by a divorce, the loss of a job, or a death in the family, the children should understand what's going on. Keeping them in the dark or smoothing over the details will only increase their anxiety. The more frank you are, the more your children will be encouraged to be honest with you about their feelings.

★ **Don't hide your doubts about the move.** By all means point out the advantages of where you'll be moving, but don't forget to give your children the idea that it's normal to be sad about leaving their old life behind. Let them know that you, too, have some regrets about moving. On the other hand, don't assume that all your fears are shared by your children. Some kids may adjust to moving more easily than their parents imagine.

★ **Inform your children's teachers about the move as soon as you tell the children.** If your child's classroom behavior changes, the teacher will take into account that the move is on her mind.

★ **Spend extra time with your child.** Just when there are heavy practical demands on your time, your child will need you more than ever.

★ **Allow your child to fantasize.** For many children, the idea of moving evokes powerful fantasies of a fresh start: They'll leave behind a nickname they hate, they'll always keep their room neat after the move, and so on. Even if they are unable to realize those fantasies, don't tease them about it.

★ **Read children's books about moving.** One way to help your child to work out fears about moving is to give her storybooks about kids who have moved. Ask your librarian for suggestions.

★ **Help ease your child's fears about leaving old friends.** Children worry that when they move, their old friends will forget them. Many of the projects in *Goodbye, House* are designed to give children the sense that the move doesn't mean that their past life is irretrievably lost. Here are some ways you can help:

1. Suggest to your child that she keep in touch with old friends. *Goodbye, House* includes an address, phone number, and e-mail listing for old friends, which the child can fill out.

If you're moving a short distance, let her know that her old friends can come visit and that she can return to her old neighborhood. For long-distance moves, you may want to promise that she can call her best friends on their birthdays or other special occasions. If you have a family computer, e-mail is another way for your child to stay connected to her social circle.

For both short- and long-distance moves, we've suggested that your child give friends prestamped postcards (available at the post office) with her name and address. That way, she can be sure to get some mail during her first weeks at her new home.

2. Encourage your child to say goodbye to special people. Children who are normally outgoing may have an attack of shyness when they are moving. They may need encouragement, but they will feel better if they make the effort to say goodbye to people like their school-bus driver and soccer coach. You might also want to let your child pick out a small gift for people who have been especially nice, such as a favorite baby-sitter or neighbor.

3. Plan a going-away party. Some teachers are amenable to having a party in the classroom at the end of the school day if the parents supply the snacks and drinks. Or you may choose to have a party at home. Some families like to have a farewell open house for both kids and adults before the move. Take pictures of your child and her friends at the party. Later she may want to paste them into *Goodbye, House*.

4. Lend or give your child an inexpensive camera. For some projects in *Goodbye, House*, we've asked your child to paste in a photograph. A picture of where you live now, for instance, should be a comforting reminder during the first few weeks at the new home. You may already have photographs on hand to paste into *Goodbye, House*.

★ **Prepare your child for whether his pets will move or not.** If the pet will be making the move with you, decide with your child how the pet will be cared for during the move. On moving day, your child may want to be responsible for keeping the dog or cat out of the movers' way. Enough people have told of a pet panicking and running off on moving day that it seems clear that pets sense the impending move and need the special attention your child may provide.

If you're moving to a place where pets are not allowed or if they can't come with you for some other reason, explain the situation to your child and discuss what would be best to do. Are there friends or relatives who might like the pet? Once a new owner is found, allow the child to be present when the transfer is made. If possible, let him see where the pet will be staying. Your child may want to write instructions for the new owner explaining how to take care of the pet. He can also give the new owner a postcard to write news of the pet's well-being.

★ **Make lists with your child** of ways she can help out before the trip, on the day of the move, and once you arrive at the new home.

★ **Allow your child to participate in cleaning out and packing.** And remember the two cardinal rules for cleaning out: (1) Don't throw away any of your child's possessions without asking. He may decide to give them away or to sell them in a yard sale, but let the decision be his. The space you save in the packing just isn't worth the upset. (2) Don't leave anything behind—including a swing set that's impossible to move, or a piano that can't fit through the door—without first explaining to your child before the move. He may want to take pictures of the things he loves that won't be coming with you and paste them in *Goodbye, House.*

Encourage your child to pack his own toys and belongings. Be sure to label the carton so it can be found easily when you arrive.

★ **Make plans with your child for moving day.** To have the kids around or not to have them around on moving day…that is the question. The move might be a lot easier if they were at a friend's or relative's house. But some children might feel neglected. So talk with each child to see how he or she feels and if and how you can accommodate these feelings.

If your children will be there on moving day, sit down beforehand and make a list of simple chores they'll be responsible for. The children will feel that they're needed and you'll feel relieved that they won't be getting in the way.

★ **Consider the children's interests when packing the moving van.** It may be worth considering whether you'd like the movers to put your children's furniture and belongings in the van last so they can be the first to be taken out on arrival. Getting the kids' rooms set up first not only reassures them that they have a "home" in the new house or apartment but—on the practical side—gives them a place to stay out of the way. They can be involved in arranging their rooms while you oversee the rest of the unloading and unpacking.

★ **Celebrate your arrival.** Children have a real sense of ceremony. Perhaps you can arrange to have a special toast when you first arrive at your new home—champagne for the adults and milk and cookies for the kids.

★ **Let your child help decorate her room.** If you can arrange to give your child a fair amount of autonomy in this process, it will help her gain a sense of mastery over her new environment. For instance, if the rooms are to be painted, allowing your child to help choose the color of her room might make her happy. You might want to promise her a new thing for her room, such as a new bedspread or a big bulletin board.

★ **Help your child make new friends.** The biggest fear about moving is that the new kids won't like them. Each child has his own pace when making new friends and becoming familiar with the neighborhood. Some kids are eager to start. Others need more time. Whatever the pace of your child, respect it and don't push too hard. You can help best by being available to facilitate the process. On that score, here are some suggestions from children:

1. Many children say it's awkward to walk over by themselves and knock on a neighbor's door to see if there are any kids to play with—and it may not be wise to let your child go alone since you won't know much, if anything, about your new neighbors. It's a good idea to go with her and introduce yourself to your new neighbors while she meets the children in the house. Encourage her to invite new friends over, even if the condition of the house is less than perfect.

2. Very often the excitement of the moving van will bring neighborhood kids over to see what's going on. If possible, have lemonade and cookies on hand.

3. Children report that one of the best ways to get to know a new neighborhood is to bicycle or take a walk with a neighborhood child. The new neighborhood friend can point out where other children live and play. Some children say it's helpful if a neighborhood friend draws a map for them.

4. As was true before the move, children need your special attention after the move, too. More story time before bed, walks and drives together to explore the area—all will help reassure your child that, no matter what, he's still got you.

5. The more social networks you set up, the better for your child. If you join a church or synagogue, the children can start going and making friends there. Joining the local Y can bring the entire family into contact with new people. Joining the parents' organization at your children's school will help them feel you're a part of their community. By meeting parents of children the same age as yours, you will begin to develop a network of people to ask about clubs, scouting programs, Little League, and other activities that you think your children might be interested in.

★ **Help your child prepare for the first day of school.** Whether your child arrives during the school year or begins school with the rest of the children, the first day of school can be frightening. There are things you can do in advance to help make the first day of school as problem-free as possible.

1. Try to arrange to go with your child to meet his teacher before the first day of school. Then he can see the classroom and get a sense of the layout of the school, and the teacher can show him some of the books he will be using and what he will be studying. Also, by finding out something about your child in advance, the teacher will be better able to introduce him to the class. The more the teacher can tell the class about your child, the more questions the other kids can ask him about himself.

2. Depending on your child's age and needs, you may want to accompany her on the trip to school for the first few days. Or an older brother or sister or a child in the neighborhood could take her.

3. Check your child's progress in school during the first few months. If there are any problems, talk with the teacher. You might decide to arrange for special help so he can catch up in subjects in which he may be behind.

Eventually your child will make friends and settle into her new home and school. By then, "where we used to live" will be a warm memory to be recalled with pleasure. Once the adjustment is made and *Goodbye, House* is completed, make sure that the book is kept safely so that it can be treasured along with other childhood mementos long after your child is making her own moves in the world.